Ela ⟨ :t
275 7

W9-AUY-180
www.eapl.org

31241007929071

OCT -- 2013

PICTURE WINDOW BOOKS
a capstone imprint

Editor: Julie Gassman
Designer: Ashlee Suker
Art Director: Nathan Gassman
Production Specialist: Laura Manthe
The illustrations in this book were created with watercolor.

Picture Window Books
1710 Roe Crest Drive
North Mankato, MN 56003
www.capstonepub.com

Text © 2014 Fran Manushkin
Illustrations © 2014 Picture Window Books, a Capstone imprint.
All rights reserved. No part of this book may be reproduced without
written permission from the publisher. The publisher takes no
responsibility for the use of any of the materials or methods described
in this book, nor for the products thereof.

Library of Congress Cataloging-in-Publication Data
Manushkin, Fran.
 Sincerely, Katie: Writing a letter with Katie Woo / by Fran Manushkin;
 illustrated by Tammie Lyon.
   p. cm. — (Katie Woo, Star Writer)
 Includes sidebars on how to write different kinds of letters and what
they need to contain.
   Summary: When Katie and her friends write thank-you letters to a class
visitor, Katie learns that writing letters can be fun.
  ISBN 978-1-4048-8126-6 (library binding)
  ISBN 978-1-4795-1921-7 (paperback)
  ISBN 978-1-4795-1887-6 (ebook pdf)
1. Woo, Katie (Fictitious character)—Juvenile fiction. 2. Chinese
Americans—Juvenile fiction. 3. Letter writing—Juvenile fiction. [1.
Chinese Americans—Fiction. 2. Letter writing—Fiction.] I. Lyon, Tammie,
ill. II. Title.
  PZ7.M3195Sin 2013
  813.54—dc23   2013004207

Printed in the United States of America in Stevens Point, Wisconsin.
032013   007227WZF13

Katie Woo

Star Writer

Sincerely, Katie

Writing a Letter with Katie Woo

by Fran Manushkin   illustrated by Tammie Lyon

"I have a surprise," Miss Winkle

said. "Today is Career Day, and we

have a guest. He's going to tell us

about his job. He is a hard worker."

"I work hard too!" said Katie Woo.

"I know," said Miss Winkle.

"After our visitor leaves, we will each write him a thank-you letter," said Miss Winkle.

Katie's Star Tip

People write letters for lots of reasons. You might want to say thank you for a gift, cheer someone up, or tell someone the latest news. You can even write a letter just to say hello!

"Hello!" said the visitor. "My name is Mr. Hample. My job is to fix things. Some folks call me a handyman."

"*Handy* is a fun word to write," thought Katie.

"I can paint your house," said Mr. Hample. "I can also fix leaks."

"I have a cold," said JoJo, "and my nose is leaking."

"I'm sorry," said Mr. Hample.

"I cannot fix your nose. But I can fix your broken windows."

"I'll remember that," said Katie.

She wrote "fixes windows."

Katie's Star Tip

Sometimes I like to make notes before I write letters, reports, or stories. It helps me remember all the things I'd like to write about.

"Uh-oh!" yelled Pedro. "Our guinea pig got out! Can you help us find him?"

Mr. Hample did!

"I will thank him for that, for sure!" said Katie.

"Tell us more about your job," said Miss Winkle.

"Well," said Mr. Hample, "I can fix sticky doors."

"Do you mean doors with jelly on them?" asked Pedro.

"No," said Mr. Hample. "I mean doors that are hard to open."

"Oh," said Pedro. "My baby brother has sticky fingers. Our doors have lots of jelly on them."

"A little soap and water will fix that," said Mr. Hample.

Pedro asked,

"What kind of tools

do you use?"

"Sometimes

I use a wrench

and a screwdriver,"

said Mr. Hample. "I use my

brain too."

"So do I!" said Katie. "All

the time!"

After Mr. Hample left, Katie said, "Now I will write my thank-you letter."

"Great!" said Miss Winkle. "Remember, each letter begins with a heading. You can use the school's address, and the date today is February 25."

Katie's Star Tip

I am writing a friendly letter, so I just need my address and the date for the heading. If I were writing a business letter, I would also add the address of the person getting the letter. If I were writing a really close friend, I might only write the date.

First Katie wrote her name over

and over. She loved writing her name.

Then she wrote the letter to

Mr. Hample.

3827 School Way
Learning, CA 99999
February 25, 2013

Dear Mr. Hample,

Thank you for coming to our class. I know the kinds of leaks you can fix and the kinds you cannot fix. I know that you can find guinea pigs too.

You are terrific!

Sincerely,
Katie Woo

★ Katie's Star Tip

Every letter needs a greeting. I always write "Dear" with the name and a comma at the end. If you know the person really well, your greeting could be funny, like "Hey, Dude!" Or it might be sweet, like "To the best mom in the world!"

When she got home, Katie wanted to write more letters.

She wrote a thank-you note to her school bus driver. She wrote:

1610 Wooing Way
Learning, CA 99999
February 25, 2013

Dear Miss Moore,

Thank you for driving our bus.
You always know where to go,
and you never get lost.

Good for you!

Yours truly,
Katie Woo

Katie's Star Tip

The body is the heart of the letter. It's where you share news. It could be happy news or sad news or anything that's fun to tell your friends. In a friendly letter, the body sounds the way you do when you are talking. In a business letter, it sounds more serious!

Katie wrote a letter to her grandma

too. She wrote:

1610 Wooing Way
Learning, CA 99999
February 25, 2013

Dear Grandma,

It was fun sleeping over at your house. I liked making wontons with you. Can we make cookies next time?

Hugs and kisses,
Katie Woo

Katie's Star Tip

At the end of the letter comes the closing. For my grandma's letter, I used "Hugs and kisses" because it sounds sweet! Some more closings are:

Sincerely,

Love,

Yours truly,

Regards,

Katie wrote to JoJo too:

1610 Wooing Way
Learning, CA 99999
February 25, 2013

Dear JoJo,

Can I come over to your house?

Your best friend,
Katie Woo

Katie's Star Tip

The signature is the last part of your letter. I like to sign my whole name, no matter who the letter is for. But lots of people use just their first name when they write to friends and family.

"I will bring my letter to JoJo," Katie decided.

JoJo smiled when she read Katie's letter.

"You are already here," she said.

"I know!" Katie laughed. "I couldn't wait to see you."

"Letters are fun to get," said JoJo.

"I save mine and reread them on

rainy days."

Katie's Star Tip

Letters are filled with memories. People like to save them to read in the future. Did you know that letters from famous people are sometimes made into books for everyone to read? You can learn a lot about people from their letters.

Katie said, "JoJo, remember when I was home with the flu? You wrote me a nice letter. It made me feel better."

"Get-well letters are good to write," said JoJo. "I'm glad you liked mine."

JoJo's mom said, "Katie, would you like a slice of pie?"

Katie took a big bite. "It's yummy!" she said. "Should I write you a thank-you letter?"

"That's all right," JoJo's mom said. "You just thanked me."

When Katie got home, she wanted to write more letters.

"Who can I write to?" she wondered. "I have run out of people!"

As she put on her pajamas, Katie

thought and thought about it.

"I know!" she shouted. She wrote:

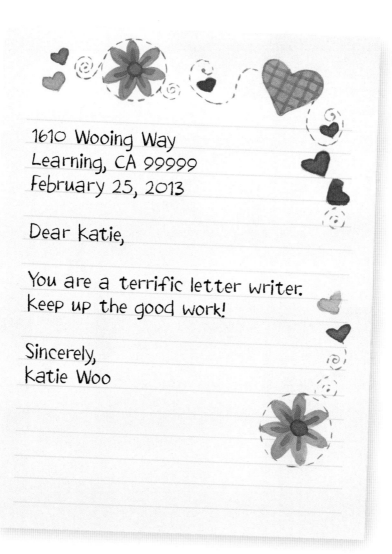

1610 Wooing Way
Learning, CA 99999
February 25, 2013

Dear Katie,

You are a terrific letter writer.
Keep up the good work!

Sincerely,
Katie Woo

That night, Katie dreamed she was writing letters to everyone in the world. It was a very happy dream!

Write your own letters!

Now that you know the parts of a letter, you can write your own. Here are a few people you might want to write to:

✿ Your grandparents: They will love to hear from you, and best of all, they will probably write you back if you ask.

✿ Your teacher: Tell him or her what you most enjoy about school.

✿ A pen pal: A pen pal is someone you can trade letters with on a regular basis. You can even find a pen pal in another country. Ask your parents or teacher to help you find one.

✿ Your favorite author: Did you know that you can often reach authors by sending letters in care of the publisher of the book? That address is usually found in the front of the book.

Glossary

body—the main part of a letter

business letter—a letter written to someone you don't know well

closing—the end of a letter

friendly letter—a letter written to someone you know very well

greeting—the beginning of a letter

heading—the part of a letter that includes the writer's address and the date; in a business letter, the heading also includes the reader's address

regards—to show respect

signature—the writer's handwritten name

sincerely—honestly or truly

Read More

Loewen, Nancy. *Sincerely Yours: Writing Your Own Letter.* Writer's Toolbox. Mankato, Minn.: Picture Window Books, 2009.

Minden, Cecilia, and Kate Roth. *How to Write a Business Letter.* Language Arts Explorer Junior. Ann Arbor, Mich.: Cherry Lake Pub., 2013.

Minden, Cecilia, and Kate Roth. *How to Write a Letter.* Language Arts Explorer Junior. Ann Arbor, Mich.: Cherry Lake Pub., 2011.

On the Internet

✿ Learn more about Katie and her friends.

✿ Find a Katie Woo color sheet, scrapbook, and stationery.

✿ Discover more Katie Woo books.

All at ... www.capstonekids.com

Still Want More?
Find cool websites related to this book at *www.facthound.com.*

Just type in this code: **9781404881266** and you're ready to go!

About the Author

Fran Manushkin is the author of many popular picture books, including *Baby, Come Out!*; *Latkes and Applesauce: A Hanukkah Story*; *The Tushy Book*; *The Belly Book*; and *Big Girl Panties*. There is a real Katie Woo—she's Fran's great-niece—but she never gets in half the trouble of the Katie Woo in the books. Fran writes on her beloved Mac computer in New York City, without the help of her two naughty cats, Chaim and Goldy.

About the Illustrator

Tammie Lyon began her love for drawing at a young age while sitting at the kitchen table with her dad. She continued her love of art and eventually attended the Columbus College of Art and Design, where she earned a bachelors degree in fine art. Today she lives with her husband, Lee, in Cincinnati, Ohio. Her dogs, Gus and Dudley, keep her company as she works in her studio.

Look for all the books in the series: